I Am...
Shout Outs!
The Book of Me!

by David Finstrom

For Monkey

Since the day you were born, I've had this idea in my mind about writing you a letter that you could reference anytime you wanted. Something that would remind you of how wonderful you make the world and how wondrous the world is in your eyes.

Turns out a letter couldn't quite cut it, so it became a book.

Dear Reader,

Make this book your own. Doodle on the pages. Add your notes and ideas. Write your name in it. Draw your own emojis, images and things that make you feel good. Add colors to enhance the page. Add more shout outs! Use it as a workbook or a diary of good thoughts. Add bookmarks on your favorite pages. Use it to push away self-doubt.

This book is all about you and how important you are to the world. It is written from your perspective (I am), because your voice and thoughts are powerful.

Never forget that you are important, and the world is a much better place because of you!

Some pages may have multiple shout outs. Other pages may have a single shout out. Either way, every shout out is for you. Read each one on the page, starting with "I Am", followed by the shout out. Take charge of them. Say them out loud. Whisper them. Make a silly voice. Use a powerful voice or hear them quietly in your head while you read. It's up to you. Have fun with them and use them to suit your style and personality. There is no wrong or right way to use this book. There is only your way.

This book of you, was written so that you could turn to any page at any time and start reading and shouting out about you! You can start at the beginning. You can start in the middle. You can start at the last page or wherever you want. You can decide to read one page at a time or read as many pages as you like. It's OK to read and reread shout outs you particularly like. It's your book to enjoy your way.

Remember, it is OK to reward yourself with thoughts and ideas that make you happy, cause you to smile and feel good. Remember, it is OK to stop and think, to relax, to reflect, and to move forward.

Most importantly, always remember, your superpower is you!

Now let's get to it...

First things first,
I Am...
Amazing!

I Am...

On a journey!

I Am...

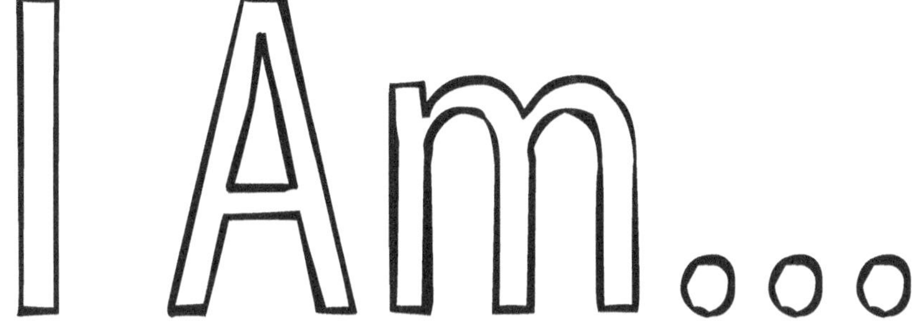

Taking it
a step
at a time!

I Am...

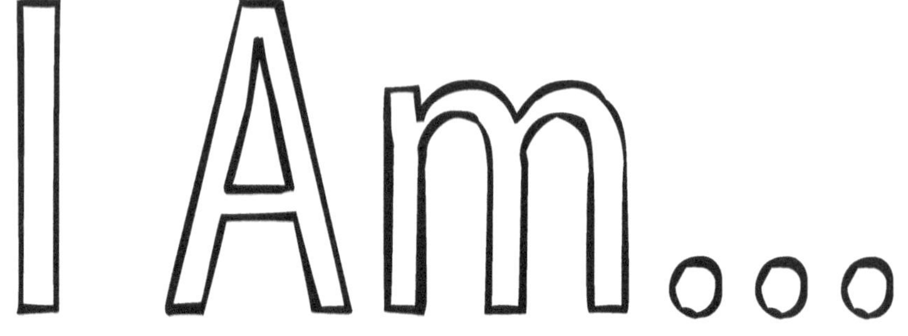

☺ Joy!

☺ Joyful!

☺ Joyous!

I Am...

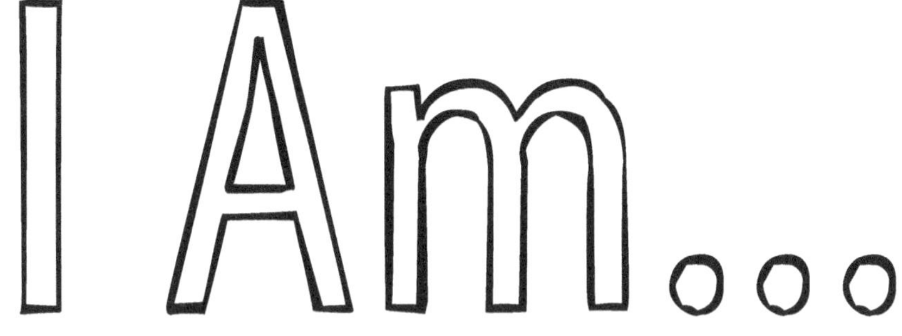

I Am... Important!

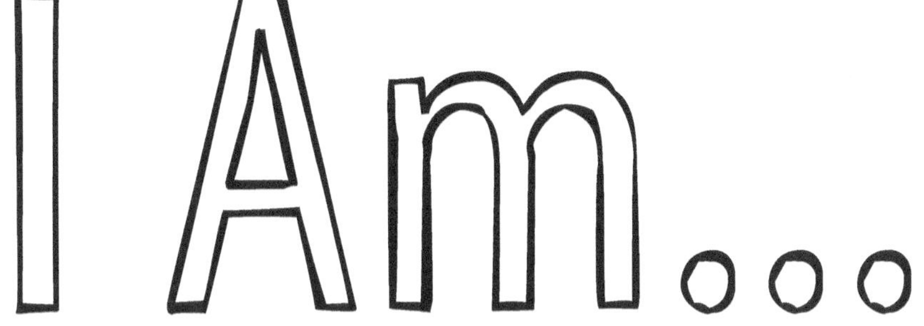

a Song!

a Dance!

a Creation!

I Am...

Music!

Artistic!

Motion!

I Am...

a Force of nature.

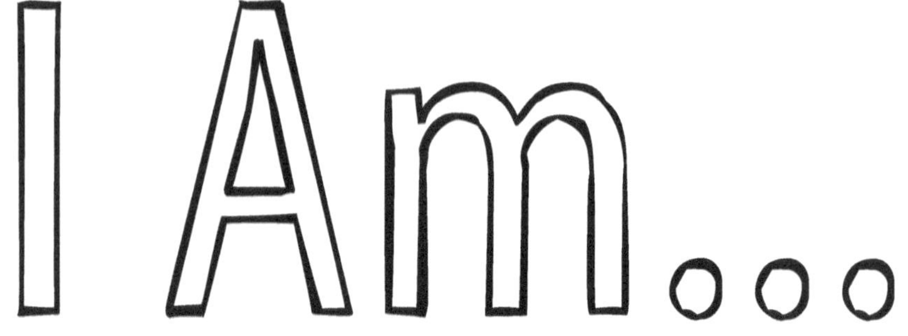

Extraordinary!
One of kind!
Unique!

I Am...

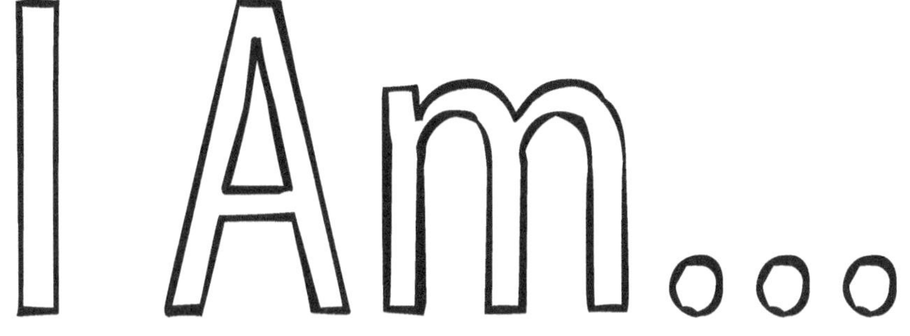

the Bee's knees!

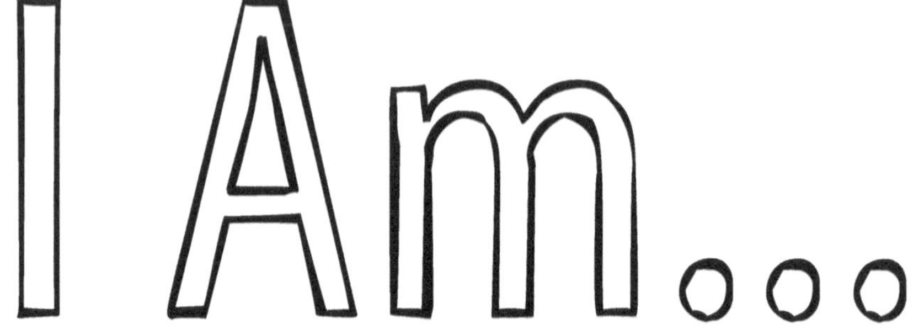

Curious!

Determined!

Excited!

I Am...

Forging
my
way!

I Am...

♡ Love!

♡ Lovely!

♡ Loving!

I Am...

Mighty!

I Am...

a Part of

something

bigger!

I Am...

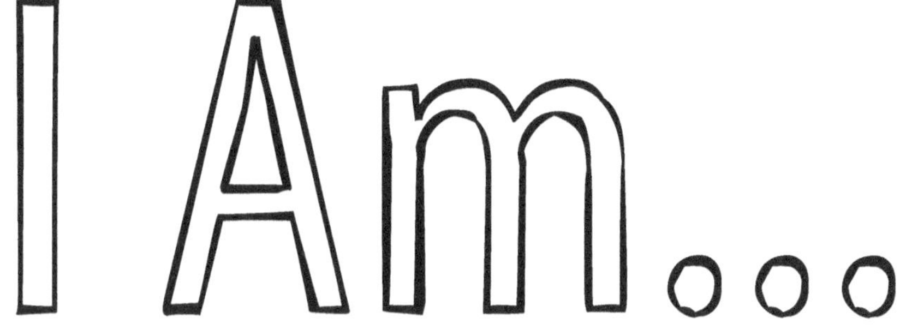

a Smile!

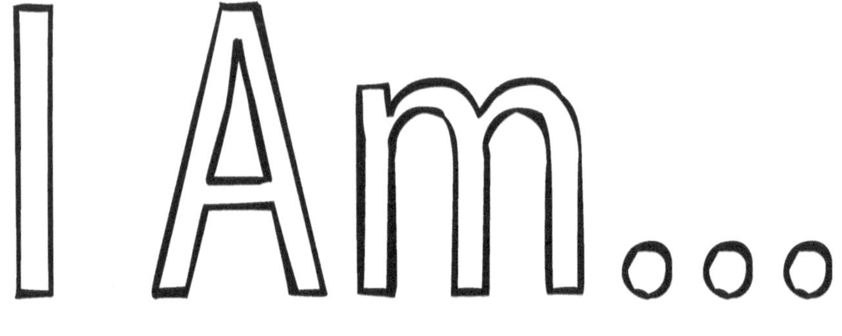

I Am...

a Friend!

Fun to be with!

Approachable!

Open minded!

I Am...

On top of
it!

I Am...

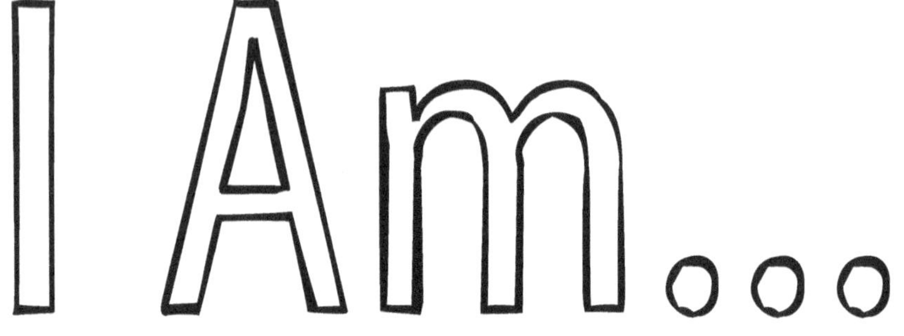

Not giving up!

I Am...

Col!

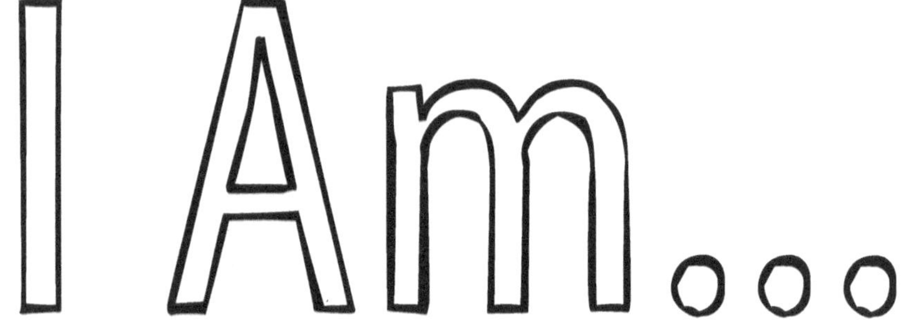

Exuberant!

Feisty!

Fierce!

Unstoppable!

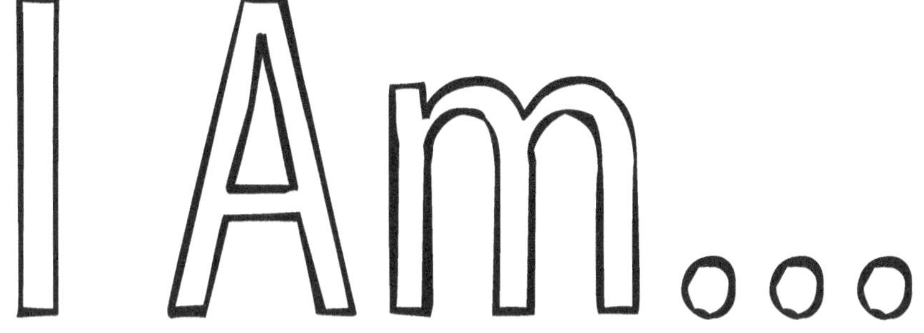

I Am...

Worthy!

I Am...

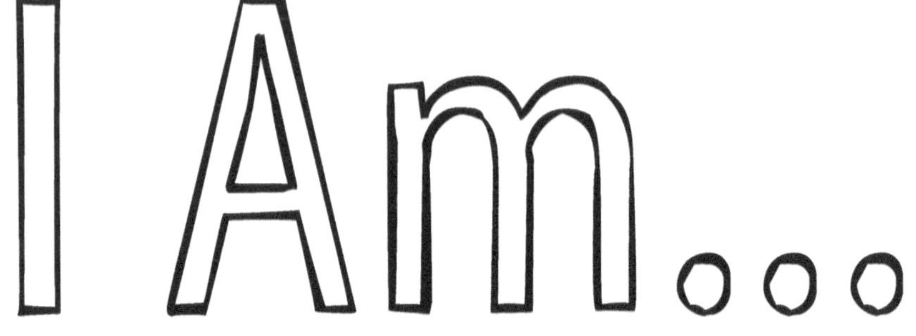

√ Incredible!

√ Relevant!

√ Significant!

√ Stunning!

Did I mention,

I Am...

I Am...

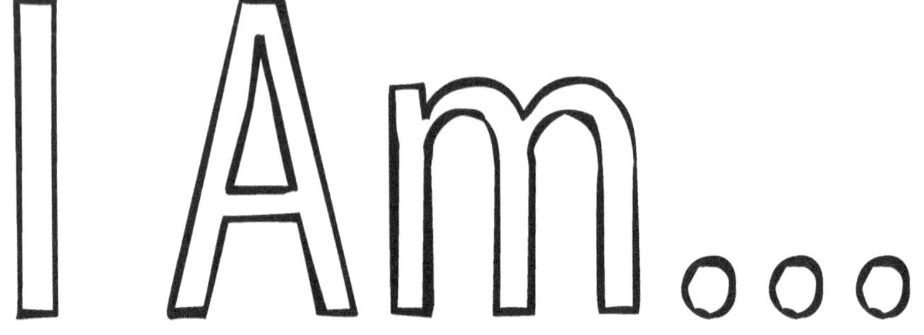

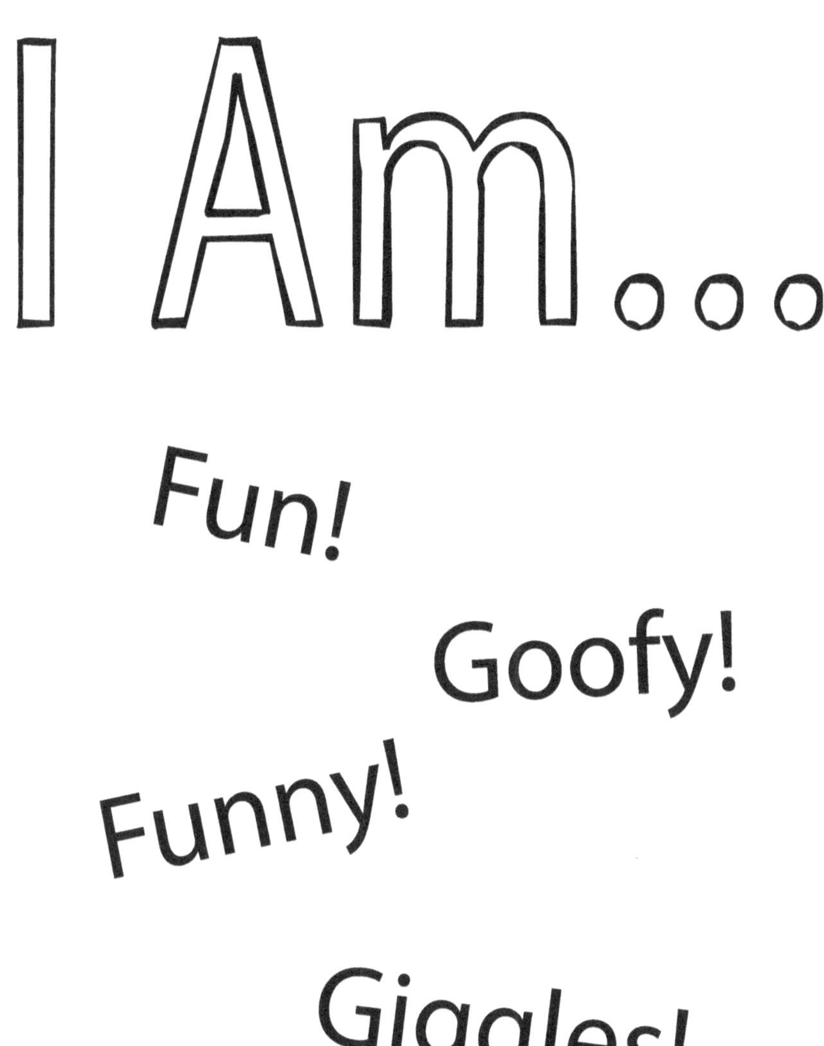
I Am...
Fun!
Goofy!
Funny!
Giggles!

I Am...

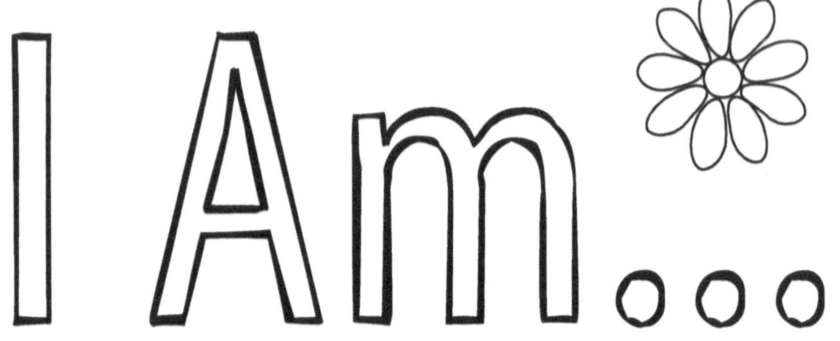

a Blessing!

a Miracle!

a Flower!

I Am...

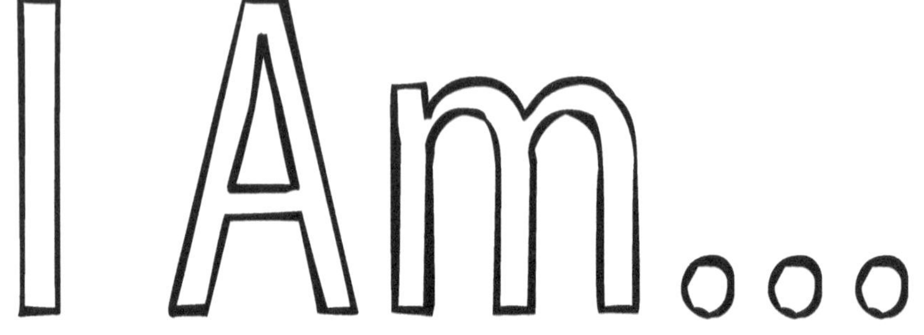

Filled with
GREAT ideas!

I Am...

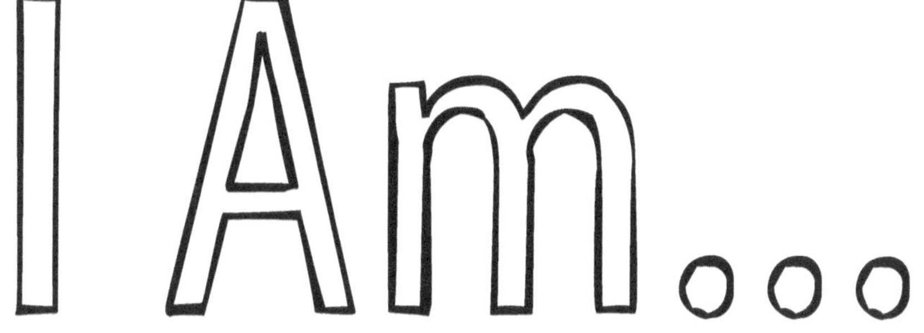

☺ Happy!

☺ Laughter!

☺ Content!

I Am...

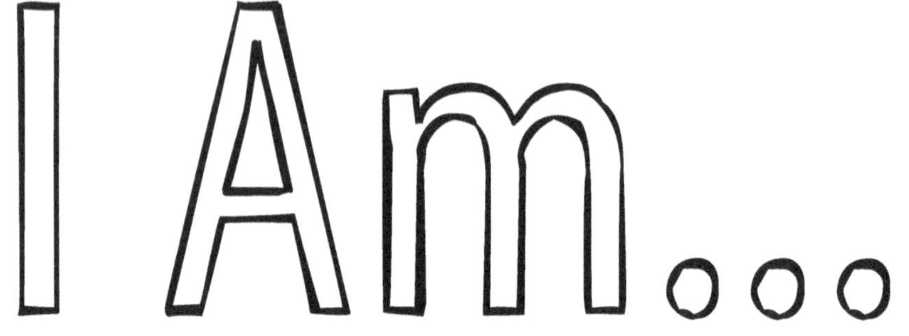

Bold!

Brave!

Courageous!

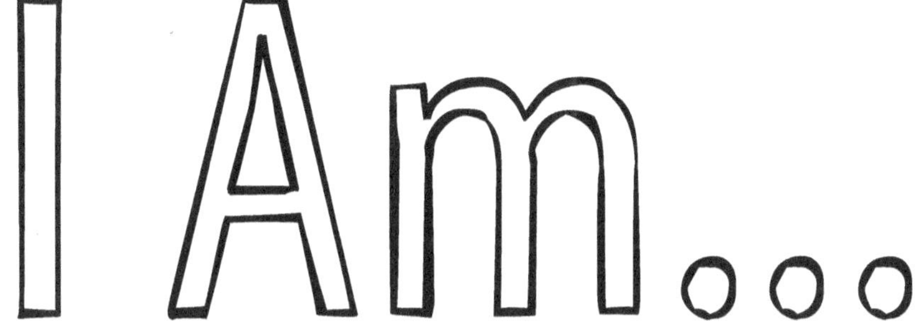

Confident!

Stellar!

Meaningful!

I Am...

Brilliant!

Sparkly!

Dazzling!

I Am...
Powerful!

I Am...

a Teacher!

a Student!

a Super Hero!

I Am...

Natural!

Resilient!

Resourceful!

I Am...

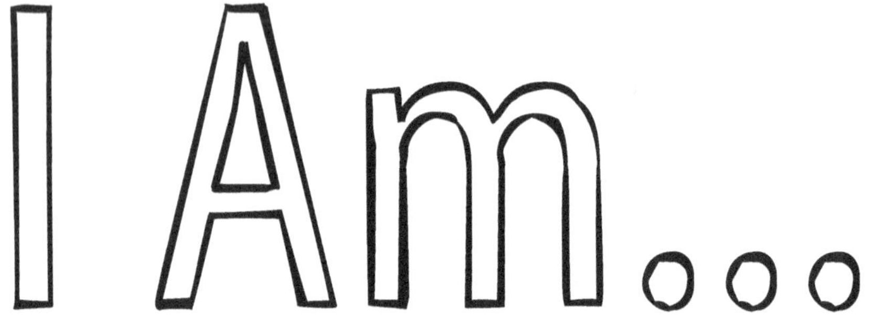

- ☐ Pretty!
- ☐ Handsome!
- ☐ Cute!
- ☐ Gorgeous!

Cherished!

Celebrated!

Encouraged!

One in a gazillion!

(1 in 1,000,000,000,000,000,000,000,000,000,000,000 x 100^3)

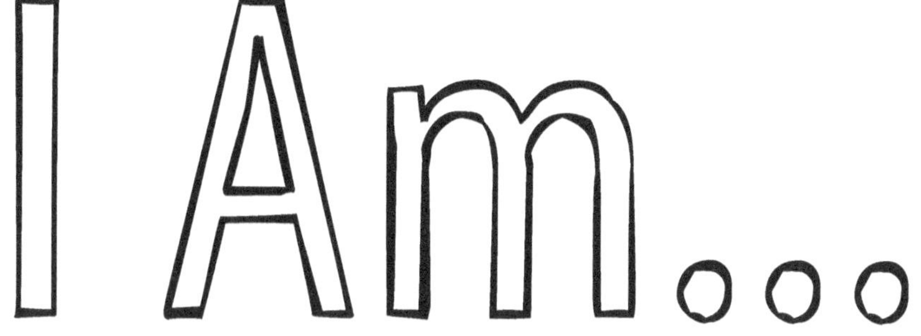

Not afraid!

Not gullible!

Not worried!

I Am...

X's and O's

XOXOX!

I Am...

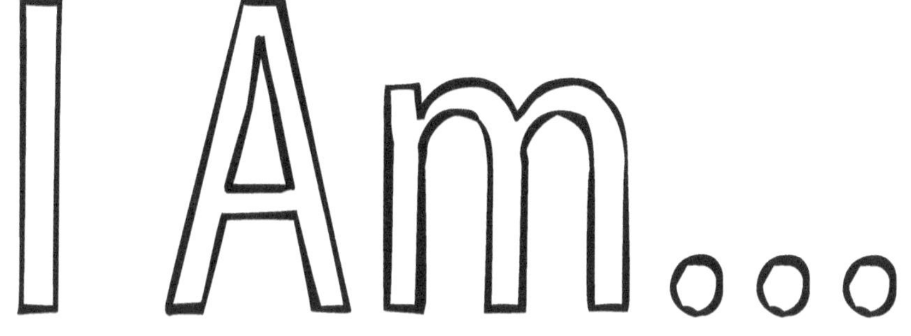

Playful!

Humorous!

Imaginative!

Observant!

Perceptive!

Aware!

I Am...
Awesome!

I Am...

Beautiful!

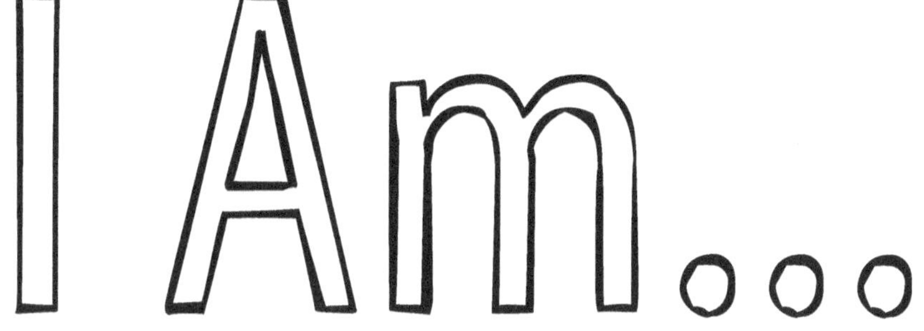

☐ Alert!

☐ Alive!

☐ Adventurous!

I Am...
a Work in progress
?

I Am...

Reaching for the stars!

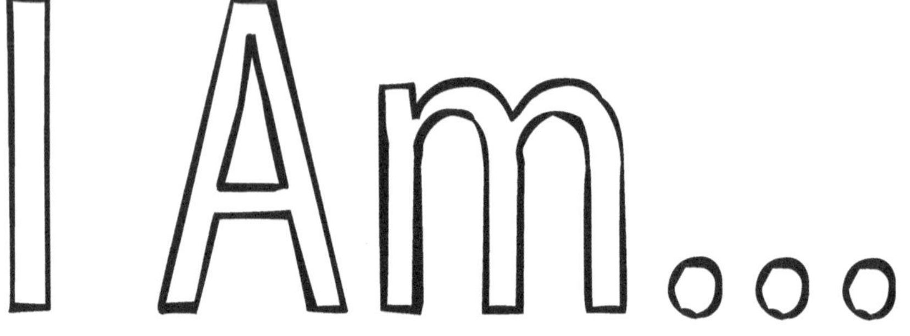

☐ Articulate!

☐ Distinguished!

☐ Versatile!

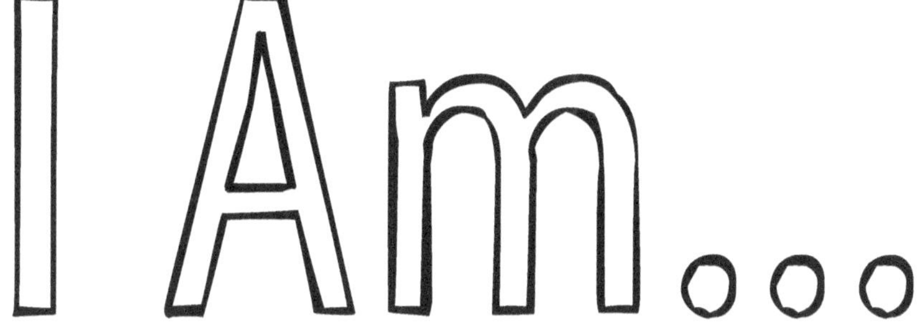

- ☐ Whimsical!

- ☐ Snazzy!

- ☐ Spicy!

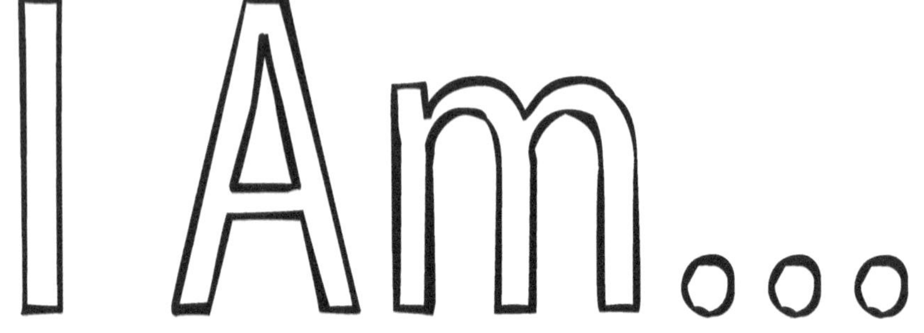

Thoughtful!

Caring!

Nurturing!

I Am...

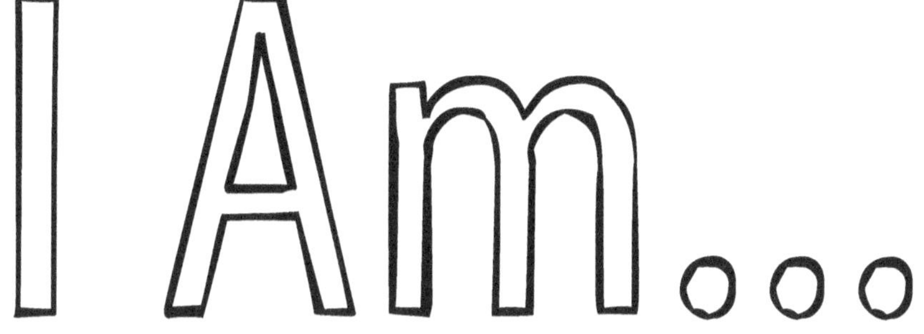

Good at what I do!

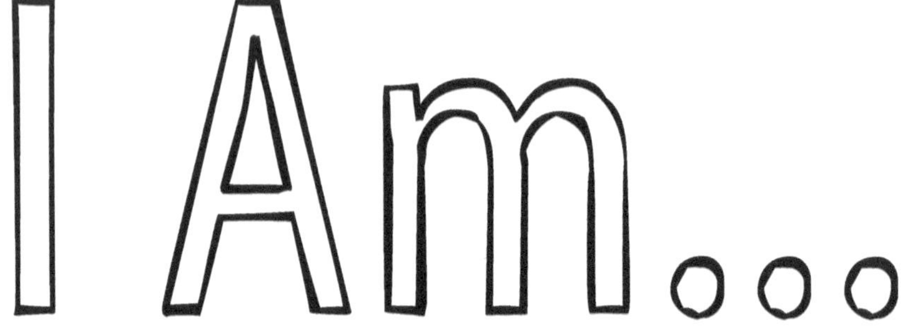

Handling it!

Working it out!

Getting there!

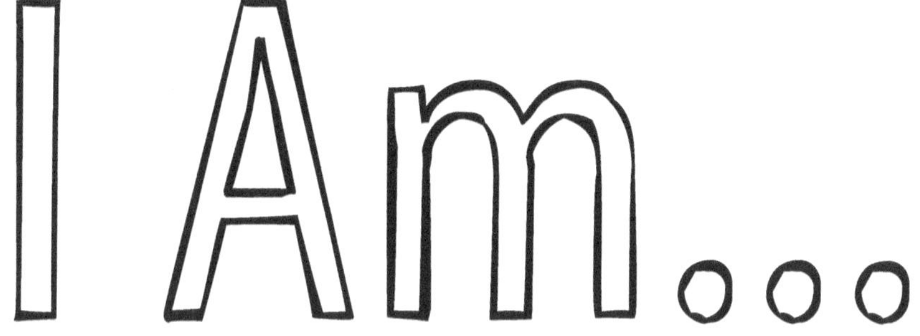

I Am...

the BEST!

I Am...

Magical!

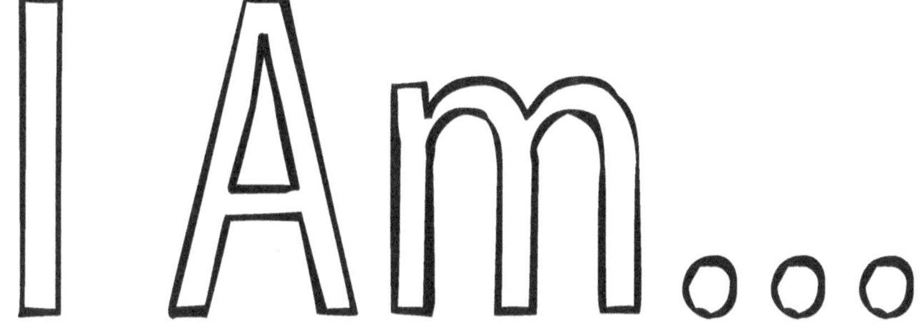

Helpful!

Giving!

a Good listener!

I Am...

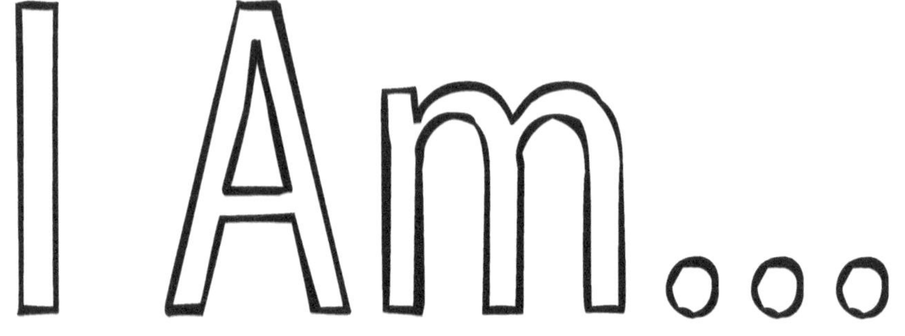

Creative!

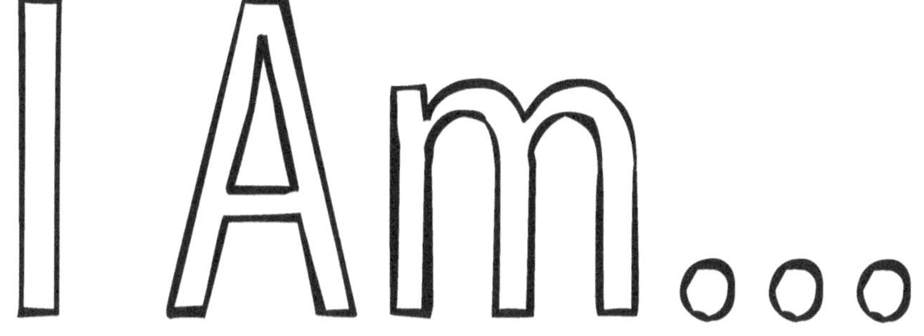

I Am...

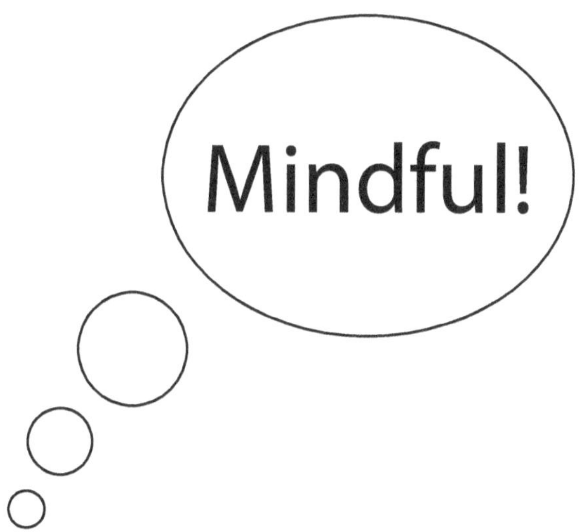

Mindful!

I Am...

Quintessential!

a Catalyst of greatness!

the G⋆O⋆A⋆T⋆!

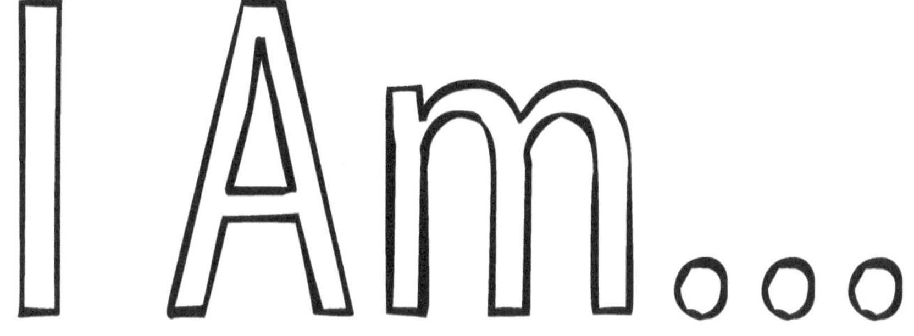

I Am...

a Rainbow!

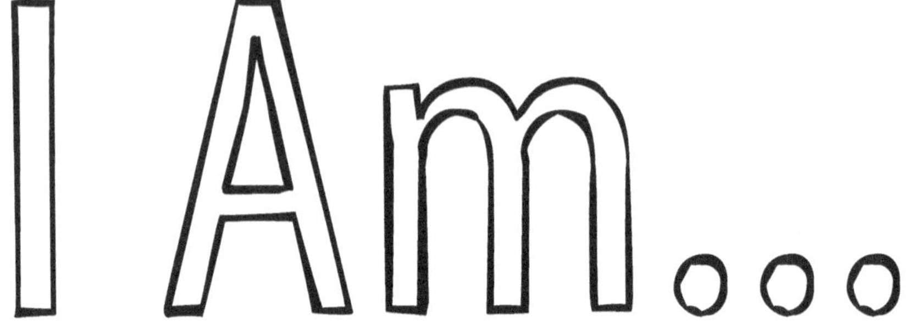

☐ Here!

☐ Ready to roll!

☐ Embracing life!

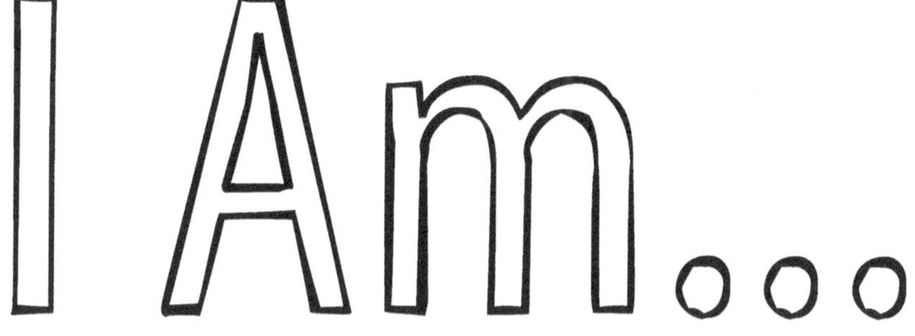

☐ Fortunate!

☐ Dynamic!

☐ Able!

I Am... Life!

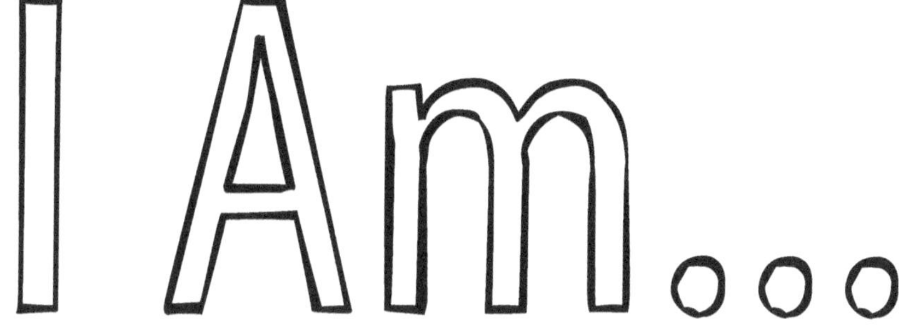

Monumental!

Magnificent!

Motivated!

I Am...

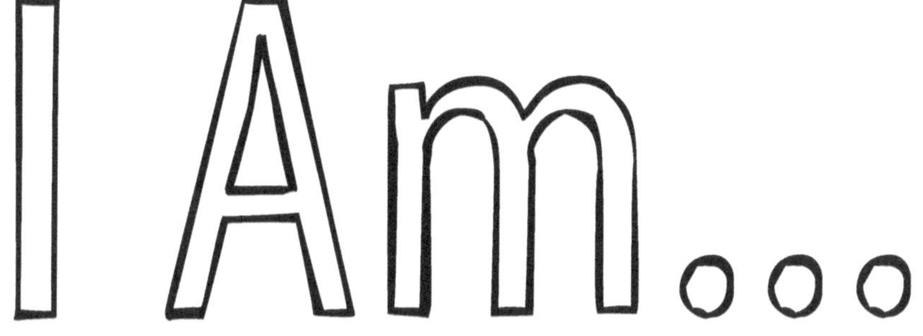

Gearing UP!
Ready to go!

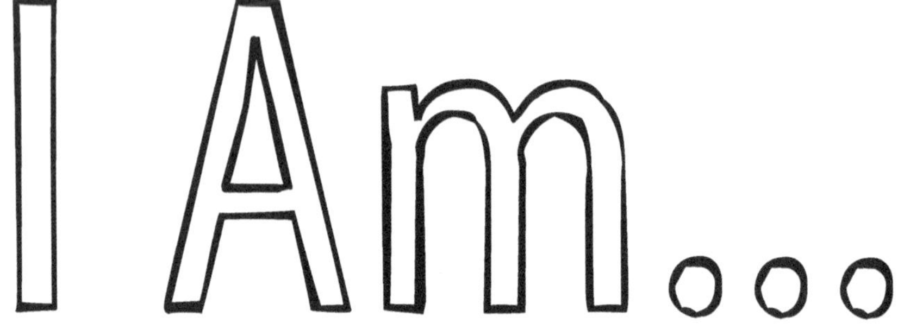

Understanding!

a Mentor!

Visionary!

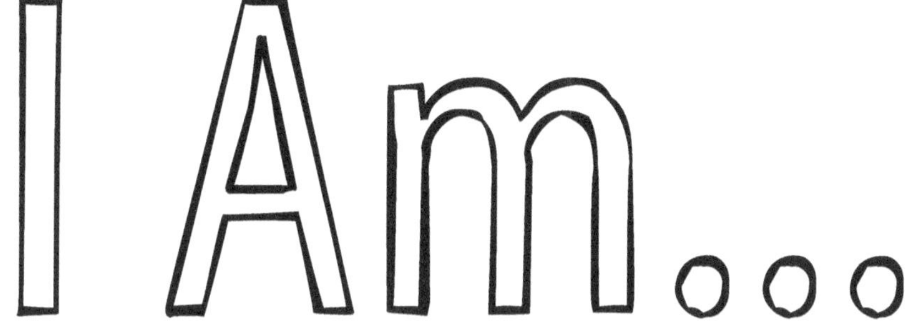

Willing!

Not afraid to try!

Going for it!

Special!
Different!
Empowered!

I Am...

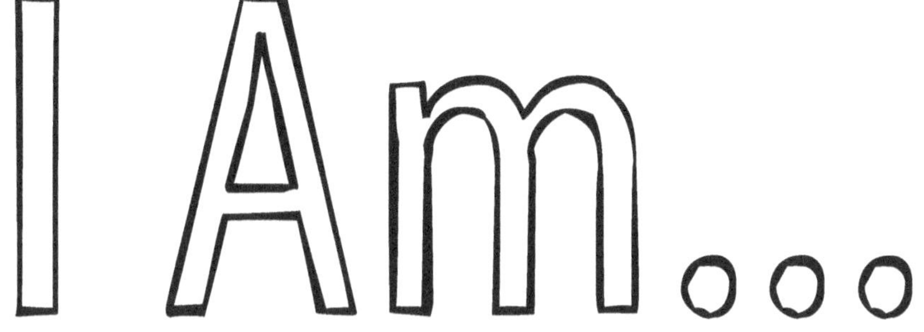

Just getting *started!*

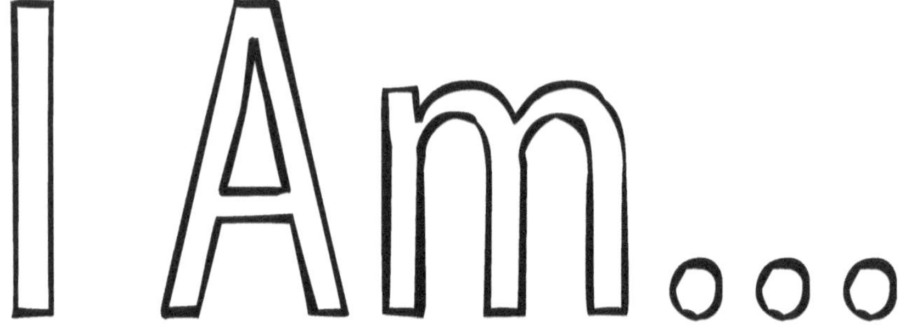

☐ Vivacious!

☐ Wild!

☐ Sensational!

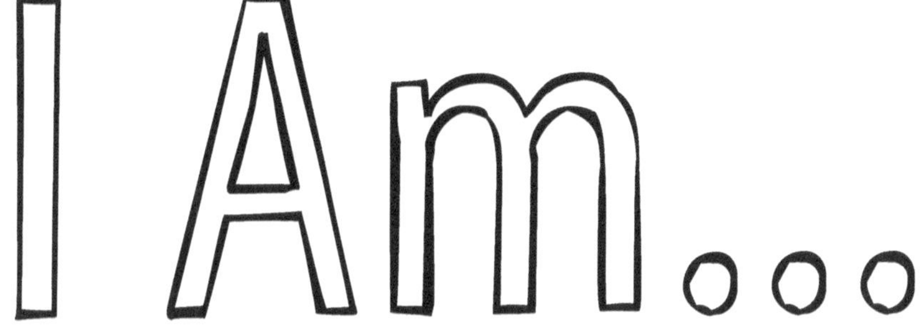

- ☐ Witty!
- ☐ Silly!
- ☐ Spontaneous!

I Am...

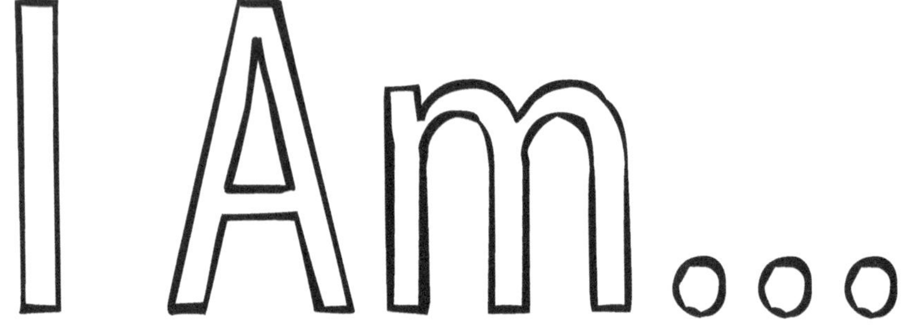

an Equal!

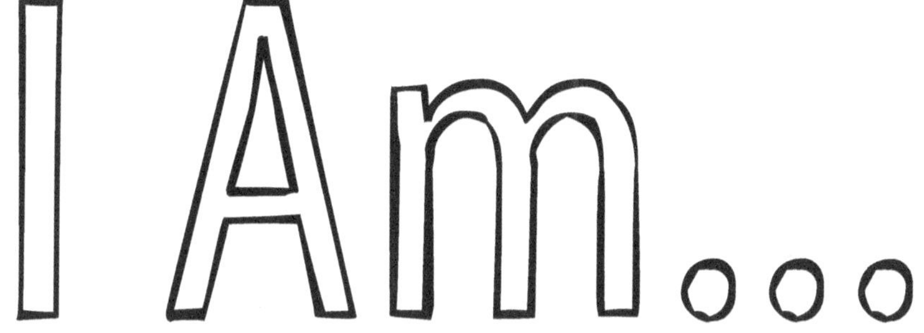

Proactive!

Making a difference!

the Community!

a Member!

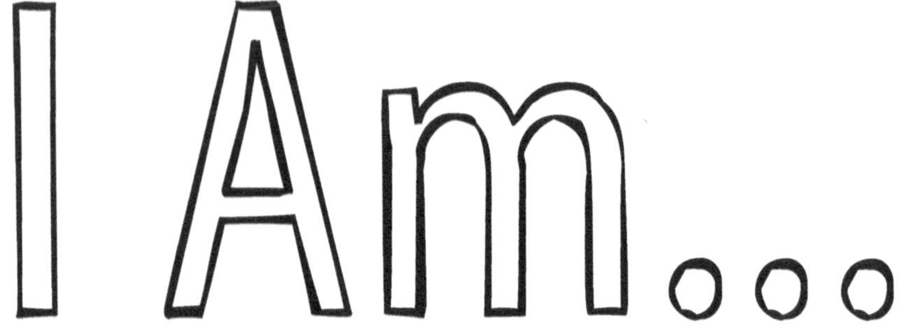

In charge of me!
Decisive!
Independent!

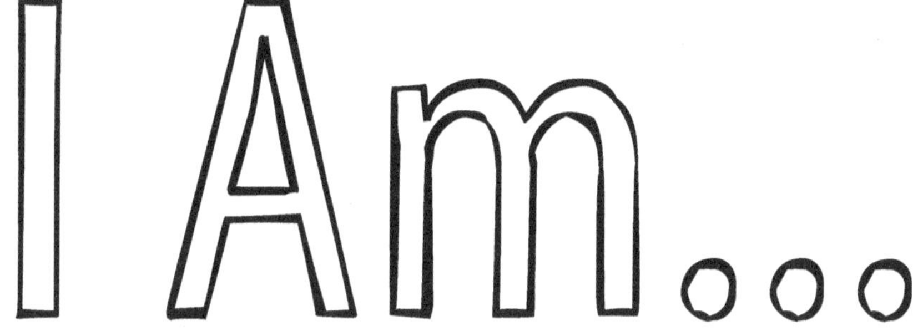

Crucial!

Focused!

Inspired!

I Am...

the Moon!

the Earth!

the Stars!

I Am...

Breathtaking!

always remember,

I Am...

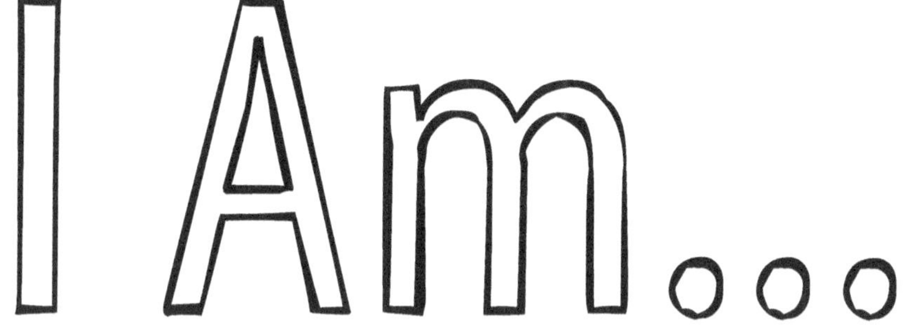

a Winner!

an Action taker!

a Go getter!

I Am...

In the
moment!

I Am...

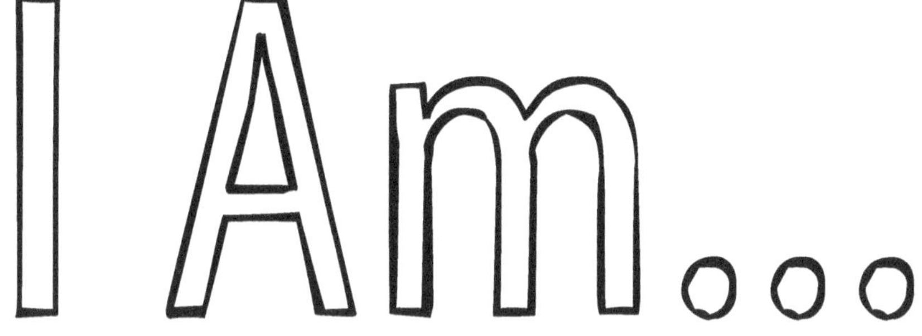

🔍 Curious!

🔍 Experimental!

🔍 Inquisitive!

I Am...

STRONG!

I Am...

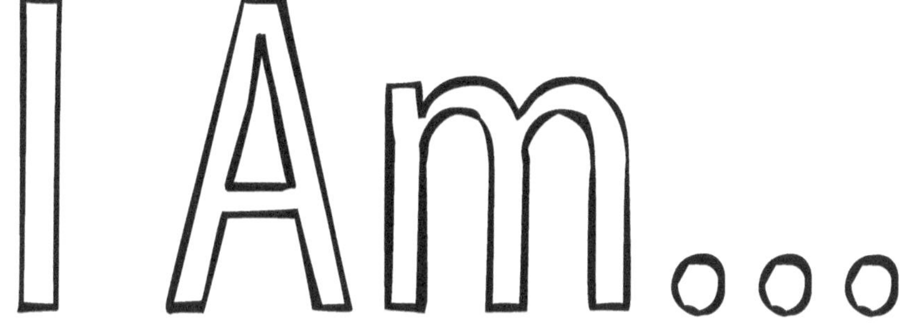

Normal!

Quirky!

Awesome sauce!

I Am...

I Am...

Zestful.

Vibrant.

Energy.

I Am...

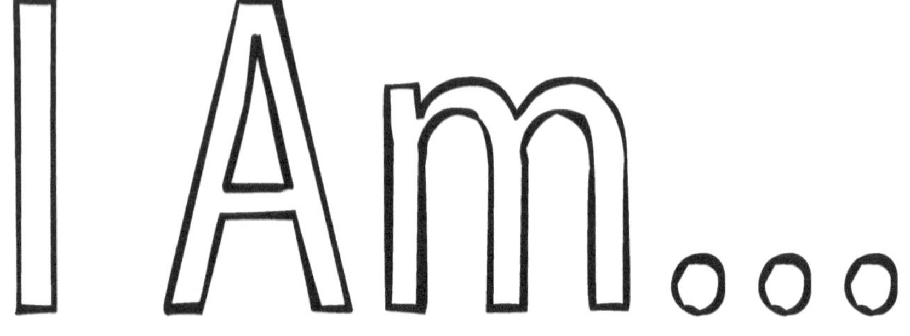

Smart!

I Am...

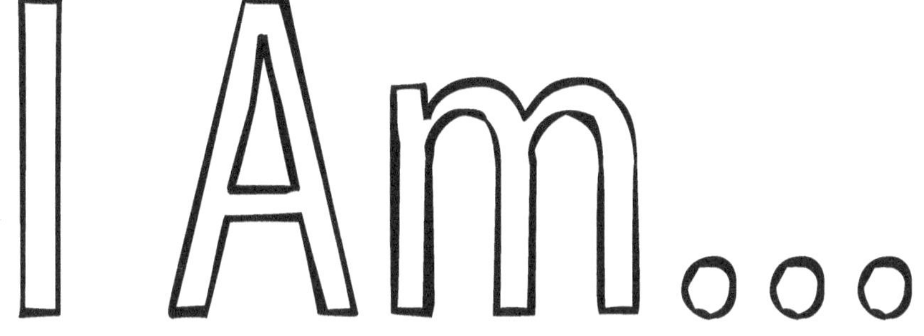

a Voice!

the Difference!

the Future!

# I Am... Well!

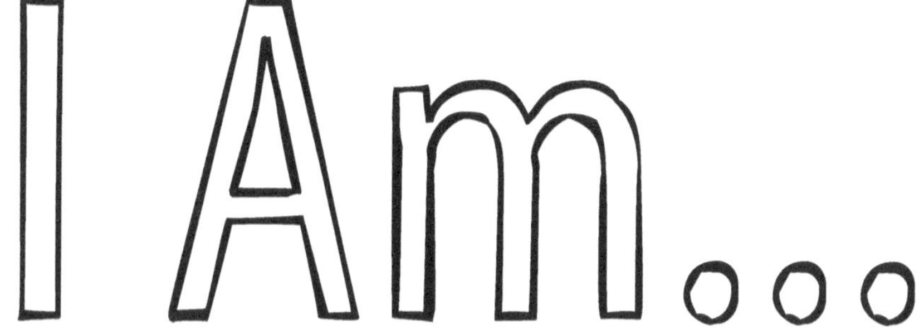

I Am...

Good!

the Rivers!
the Ocean!
the Mountains!
the Sky!

the Universe!

I Am...

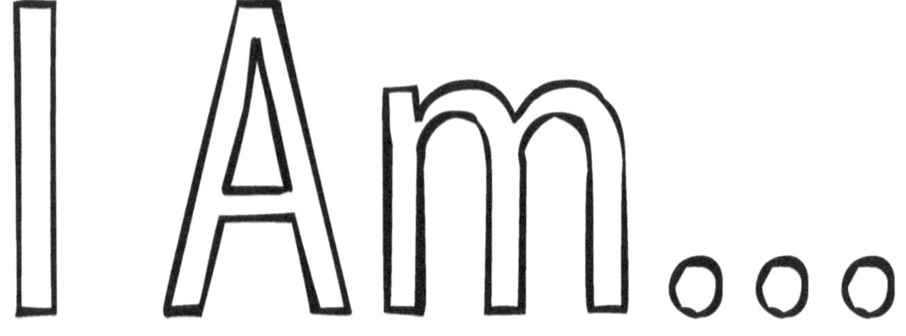

I Am...

a Work of art

I Am...

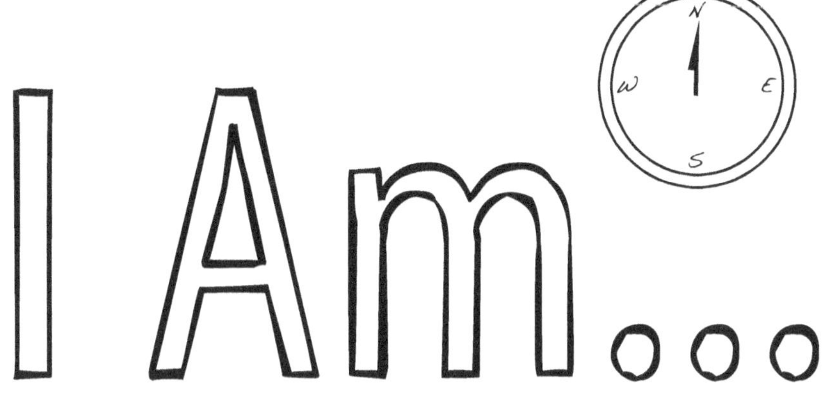

a Zenith!

an Adventurer!

an Explorer!

I Am...
OK!

I Am...

Kind!

Nice!

Empathetic!

I Am...

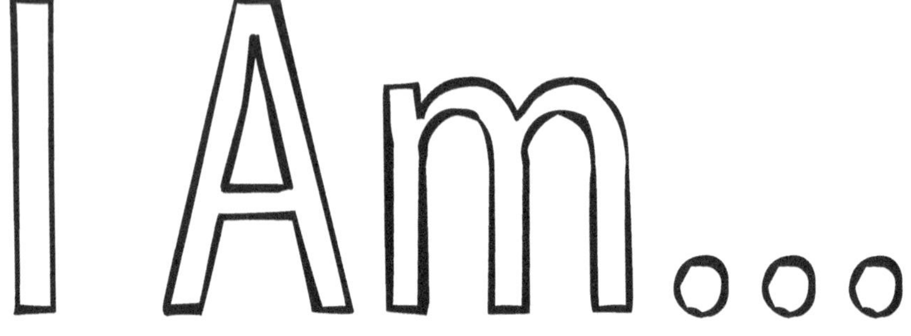

- ☐ Participating!
- ☐ Persuasive!
- ☐ Convincing!

I Am...

- ☐ Learning!
- ☐ Inventive!
- ☐ Motivated!

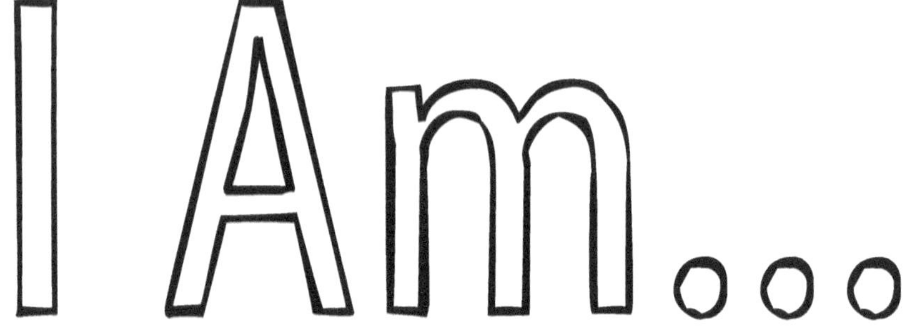

a Leader!

a Thinker!

Here to help!

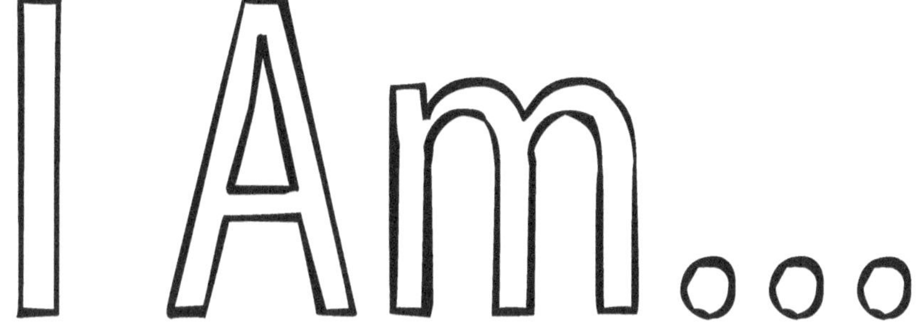

a Scholar!

Progressing!

Venturing ahead!

I Am...

Now!

I Am...

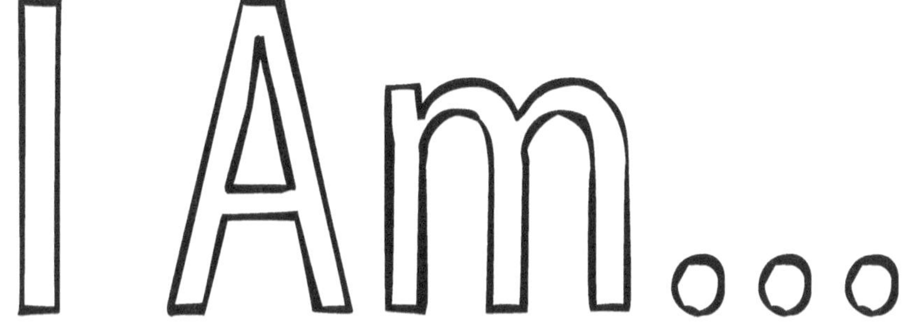

Triumphant!

I Am...

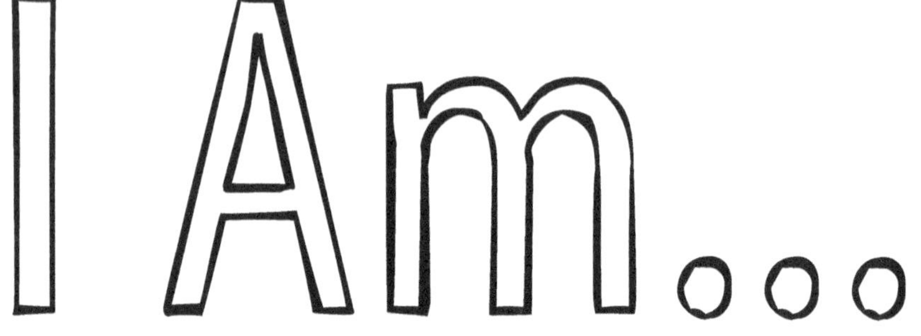

- ☐ Watchful!
- ☐ Trusting!
- ☐ Wise!

☐ Tickled!

☐ Enjoyable!

☐ Comical!

I Am...

Classy!

I Am...

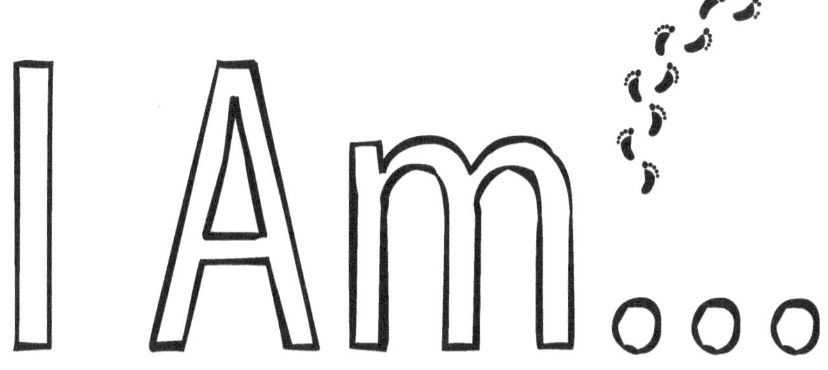

Surpassing expectations!

Reaching for the unknown!

Taking steps *forward!*

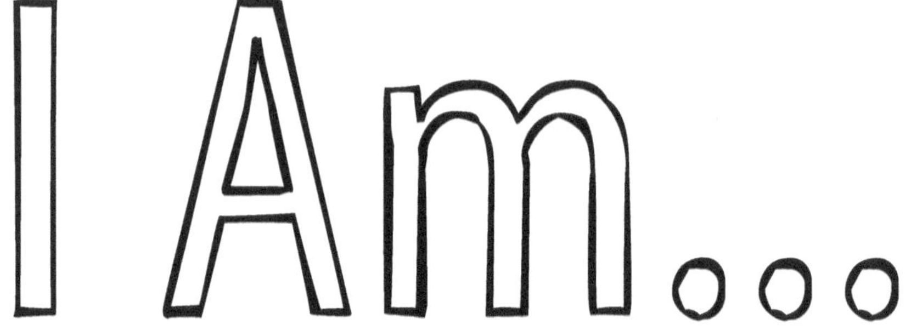

Awake!

Animated!

Attentive!

I Am...

Family!

I Am... Exceptional!

- Flexible!
- Hopeful!
- Inspiring!

I Am... Needed!

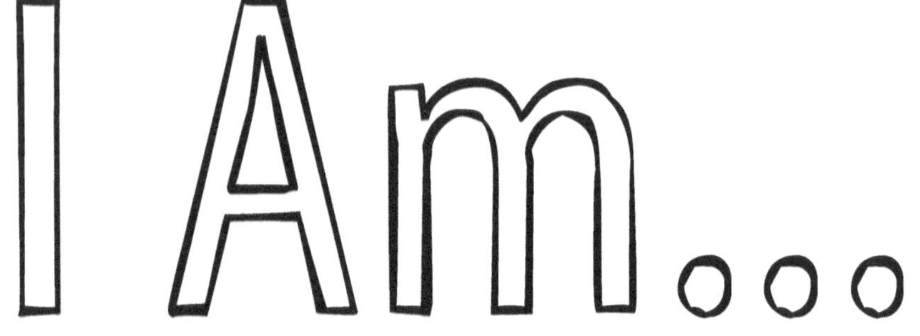

I Am...

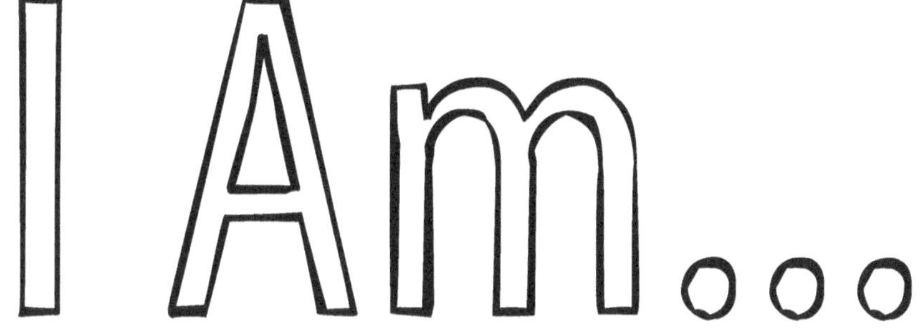

Nurturing!

Peaceful!

Respectful!

I Am...

Sensitive!

Spiritual!

Essential!

I Am...

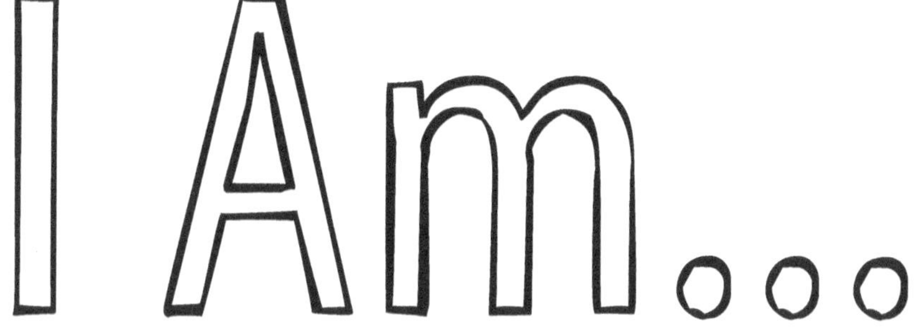

Meant to
BE!

I Am...

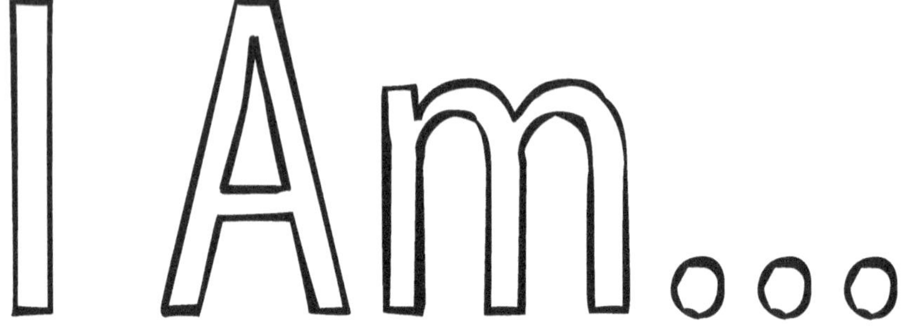

- ☐ Dedicated!

- ☐ Diligent!

- ☐ a Hard worker!

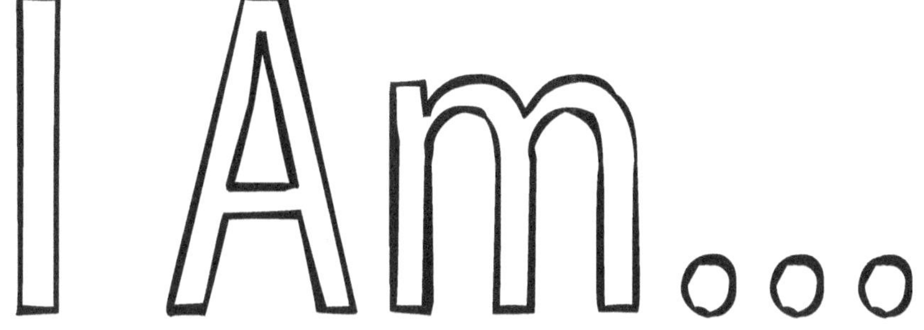

- ☐ Purposeful!
- ☐ Cautious!
- ☐ Responsive!

I Am...

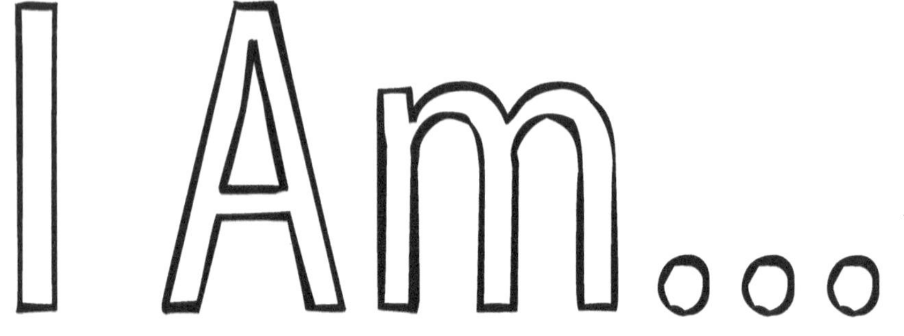

- Proactive!
- Prepared!
- Movement!

I Am...

I Am...

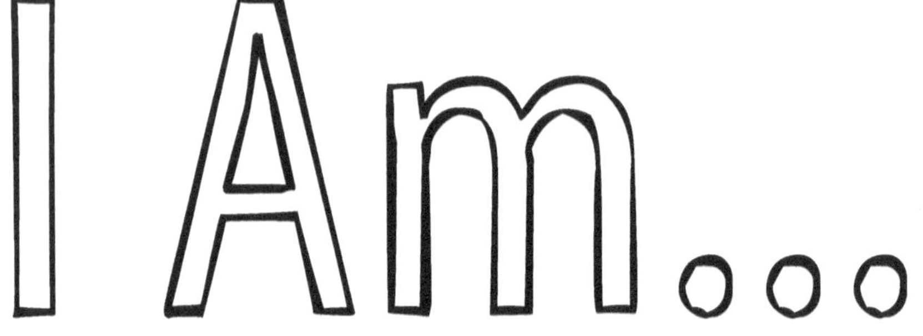

- Recognized!
- Linked!
- Connected!

I Am...

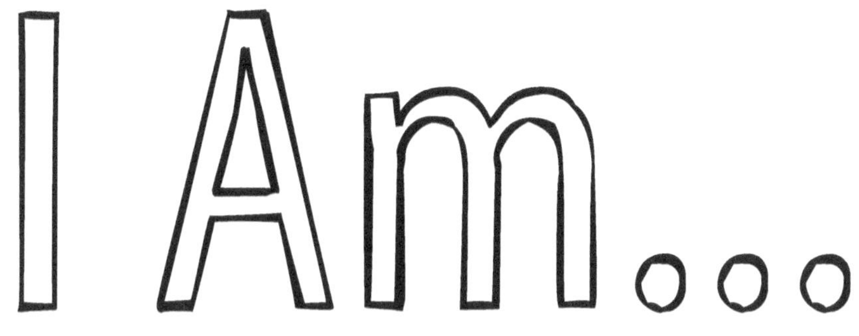

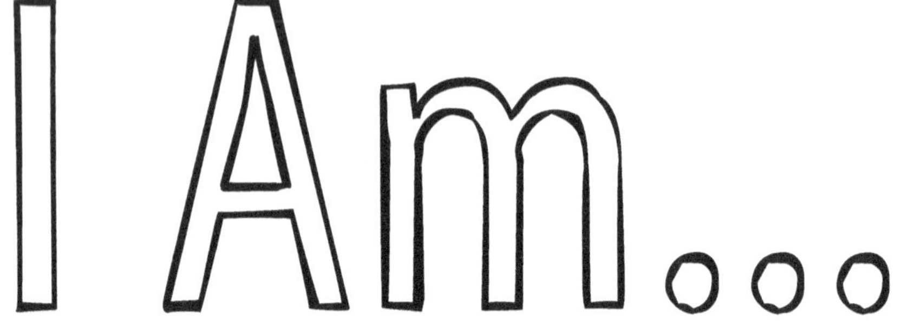

- ○ Above and beyond!

- ○ an Achiever!

- ○ In control!

I Am...

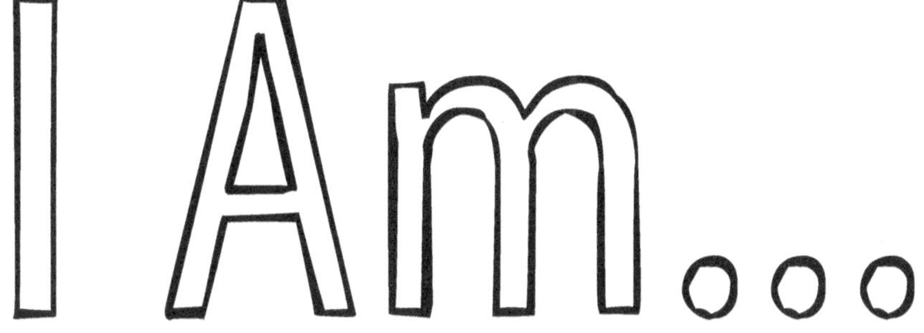

a Masterpiece!

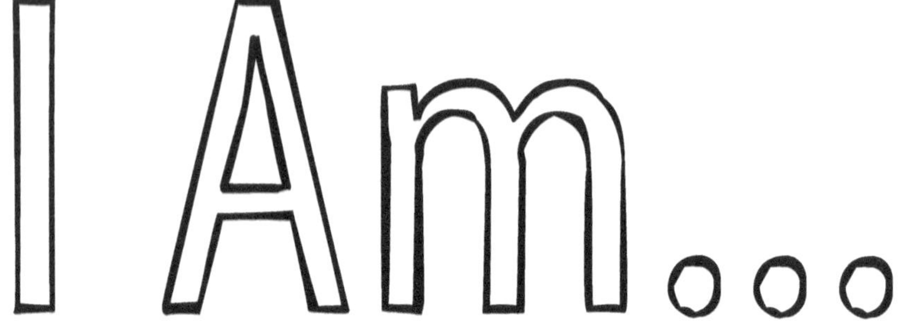

I Am...

- ☐ Futuristic!
- ☐ Retro!
- ☐ Modern!

☐ Poetry!

☐ Rejoicing!

☐ Restful!

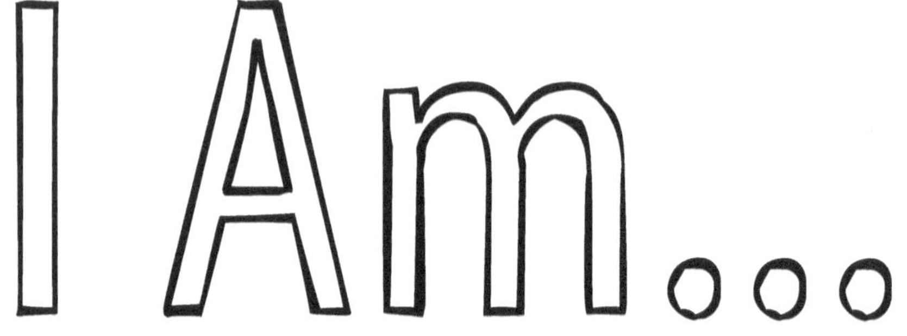

Studious!

Successful!

Knowledgeable!

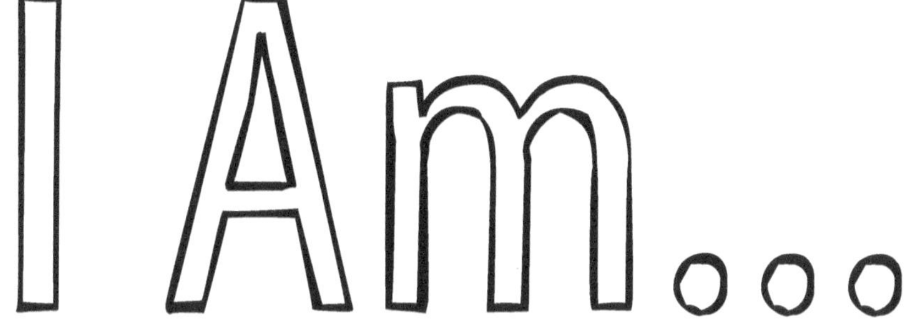

Youthful!

Wishful!

Patient!

I Am...

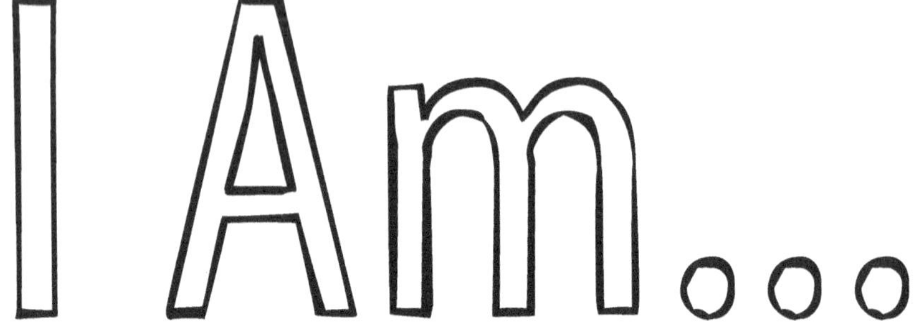

Vital!

I Am...

Active!

Illuminating!

Encouraging!

 I Am...

Everything!

Growing!

Independent!

I Am...

Lucky!

Persistent!

Responsible!

Outstanding!

I Am...

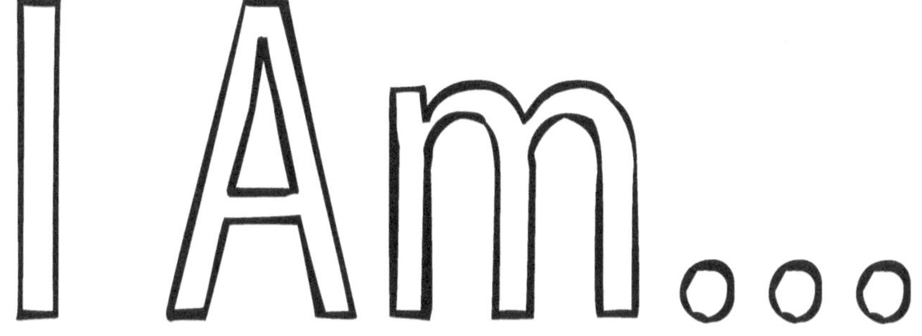

a Miracle of life!

I Am...
More!

Competent!
a Butterfly!
Complex!
Humble!
Relaxed!
Capable!
Wonderful!
Calm!
Artistic!
Simple!
Classic!
Protected!
Mysterious!

a Star!
a Storyteller!
Heard!
Original!
Down to Earth!
Breathing!
Healthy!
a Celebration!
the World!
Generous!
a Creator!
Tough!
Astonishing!

Somebody!

I Am...

Divine!

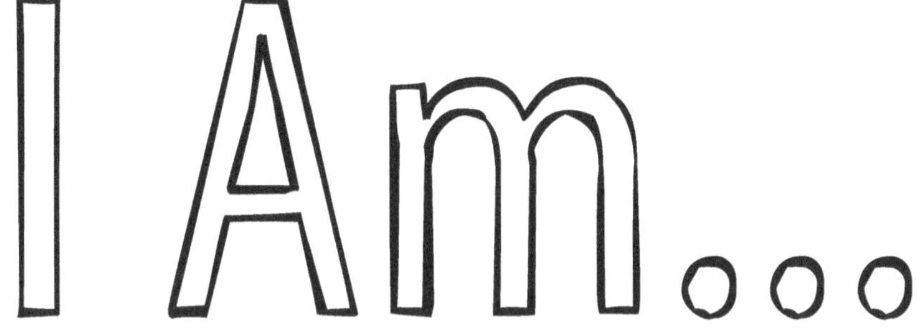

I Am...

Me!